THE BIG GREEN POETRY MACHINE

Poetic Verse

Edited By Allie Jones

First published in Great Britain in 2023 by:

YoungWriters®
Est. 1991

Young Writers
Remus House
Coltsfoot Drive
Peterborough
PE2 9BF
Telephone: 01733 890066
Website: www.youngwriters.co.uk

All Rights Reserved
Book Design by Ashley Janson
© Copyright Contributors 2023
Softback ISBN 978-1-80459-609-8

Printed and bound in the UK by BookPrintingUK
Website: www.bookprintinguk.com
YB0545Y

FOREWORD

Welcome Reader,

For Young Writers' latest competition The Big Green Poetry Machine, we asked primary school pupils to craft a poem about the world. From nature and environmental issues to exploring their own habitats or those of others around the globe, it provided pupils with the opportunity to share their thoughts and feelings about the world around them.

Here at Young Writers our aim is to encourage creativity in children and to inspire a love of the written word, so it's great to get such an amazing response, with some absolutely fantastic poems. It's important for children to be aware of the world around them and some of the issues we face, but also to celebrate what makes it great! This competition allowed them to express their hopes and fears or simply write about their favourite things. The Big Green Poetry Machine gave them the power of words and the result is a wonderful collection of inspirational and moving poems in a variety of poetic styles.

I'd like to congratulate all the young poets in this anthology; I hope this inspires them to continue with their creative writing.

NATURE WILDLIFE INSECTS EARTH RECYCLE

CONTENTS

Blair Peach Primary School, Southall

Siddique Mustafa (8)	1
Amber Ghai (9)	2
Arnav Padam (8)	4
Eshal Luqman (9)	5
Amanat Brar (9)	6
Seryn Fenandes (8)	7
Safia Mussa (8)	8
Aathuja (9)	9

Forest View Primary School, Whiteleas

Anna Vickers	10
Clintin Vacher-Allan	11
Noah Hall	12
Sophie Maxwell (9)	13
Jack Day (8)	14
Chloe Dunn	15
Ayla Mayne (8)	16
Alex Smith (9)	17
Amalie Cain	18
Daisy Fenwick	19
Archie McGann (9)	20
Ellis Cain (8)	21
Alfie Griffiths	22
Cory Speeding	23
Sydnie Corner (9)	24
Joshua Conway	25
Boux Sanderson (9)	26
Ilayda Erol	27
Summer Riley	28
Lisa Krajewski	29
Logan Cooper	30

Hamilton College, Hamilton

Shannon Olusola-Johnson (11)	31
Ethan Akun (10)	32
Aryaman Reddy (10)	34
Rebecca Coughlan (10)	36
Benjamin Psaila (10)	38
Oreoluwa Akinkugbe (10)	40
Bella Babalola (10)	42
Flynn Thomson (10)	43
Rafe Chesworth (10)	44
Jorja Smith (10)	45
Blyth Robertson (10)	46
Tafara Mutezo (10)	47
Max Boyd (10)	48
Blair Kinnoch (10)	49
Kathleen Bullen (10)	50
Caleb Browning (10)	51
Isaac Jalil (10)	52

Lakeside School, Chandler's Ford

Logan Barter (11)	53
Archie Greaves (10)	54
Koby Bartlett (11)	55
Dexter Wyeth Whitfield (11)	56
Leon Cawley (10)	57

St Margaret's CE Primary School, Great Barr

Halimah Hussain (10)	58
Harlem Hendra-Smith (10)	59
Sarah Kouevi (10)	60
Jiya Jagpal (9)	61
Isabelle Shakespeare (9)	62

Ariyanna Turner-Rathbone (10)	63
Eliza Flora (10)	64
Jovan Jagpal (9)	65
Dhiren Flora (9)	66
Finley Mcdonald (10)	67
Skye Clarke (10)	68
Matilda Johnson (9)	69
Arvind Singh Bains (10)	70
Harley Morris (9)	71
Amirah Shaikh (9)	72
Alfie Fowler (9)	73
Katie Shaw (10)	74
William Pedley (9)	75
Olivia Bell (9)	76

Suffah Primary School, Hounslow

Musa Ghalib (10)	77
Yasirah Aaidah (10)	78
Syeda Aliya Ahmad-Shah (11)	80
Muhammad Bashir (11)	81
Asma Mohamed (11)	82
Muna Abdelrahman (11)	84
Zaybah Sultan (11)	85
Jamal Takar (11)	86

Windermere Preparatory School, Windermere

Elizabeth Johnson (11)	87
George Allen (11)	88
Jonah Lewis	90
Louis Bromley (11)	92
Oliver Gale (11)	94
Eve Wearmouth (11)	96
Harry Owens (11)	98
Verity Larkins (11)	99
Natalee Rowe	100
Vincent Koenig (10)	101

Woodland Community Primary School, Heywood

Leo Robinson (10) & Maja Grodzka (11)	102
Mylo Ferns (10)	104
Jaydan Clegg (11)	105
Athanasios Karanikas (10)	106
Lacie Keefe (11)	107
Isla Ashton (9)	108
Madison Matthews (9)	109
Matylda Knach (10)	110
Logan Done	111
Dominik Stankowski (10)	112
Charlie Lees (9)	113
Archie Green (9)	114
Jemima Lokongo (8)	115
Lola Barlow (9)	116
Harley Burgess (9)	117
Egor Konyshev (9)	118
Jacob Sutton	119
Lillie Sigsworth (11)	120
Asiya Abiona (10)	121
Oliver Lyons-Butler (10)	122
Lucas Newton (10)	123
Kaleb Innes (10)	124
Leo Haycock (11)	125
Kai Haslam	126
George Heslop (9)	127
Jenson-James Cooke (10)	128
Theodore (8)	129
Ayla	130
Tommy Harman (10)	131
Robyn Murphy (8)	132
Alicja Roczen (10)	133
Shaniya Derbyshire	134
Anum Ansari (9)	135
Anastasia Czyżewska (9)	136
Laceymai Maher	137
Katelyn Brewin (8)	138
Amelie Carey	139
Harry Finn (9)	140
Joshua Radcliffe (9)	141
Leo Lomax (10)	142

Obed Lokongo (6)	143
Kozen Rostmay (8)	144
AvaRose Bayleigh Sierra Mintram (6)	145
Zayan Ajaz (6)	146
Ava Mohammed (9)	147
Esme Moran	148
Sam Holt (7)	149
George Taylor (10)	150
Lola Wyderska (6)	151
Jack Harrison (7)	152
Nelly Bialous (8)	153
Kaitlin Farrell (9)	154
Isla Bradley	155
Oliver	156
Julia Bonkowska (8)	157
Charlie Howarth (7)	158
Maizie Stubbs (8)	159
Hollie Baker (7)	160
Jacob Hamilton (9)	161
Charley Cass (9)	162
Robin Gill (8)	163
Freya Jackson (7)	164
Zunaira (7)	165
Olivia Butterfield (9)	166
Logan Vilter (10)	167
Ismail Ansari	168
Isabelle Redford	169
Willow Barlow (7)	170
Salim Ouaach (9) & Marvellous	171
Alfie Hynes (6)	172
Iyosayi Ogbebor Festus (7)	173
Ameliya Hughes (7)	174
Ruby Williams (9)	175
Colby Smith (9)	176
Charlotte	177
Lainey Jackson	178
Evie Murphy (7)	179
Teejay Smith (8)	180
Jamie Wellings (6)	181
Dylan Walsh (7)	182
Jessie Sutton (6)	183
Bobby Jo Corns (9)	184
Skyla Gordon (8)	185
Skylar George (8), Nicoleta & Ella Hassan	186
Lok Ching Yan (7)	187
Gracie-Anne Curtis (7) & Kobie Keane	188
Keeyan Pike (8)	189
Lucy Hutchinson (7)	190
Nathan Barron (7)	191
Adam Hussain (7)	192
Skyla-Hart Lee-Hampson (8)	193
Carter Cleary (8)	194
Carson McKenzie (7)	195
Eleanor Jupp (8)	196
Penny Sedgley (7)	197
Matilda Sedgley (7)	198
Kai Foster (7)	199
Teca Riaquinda (8)	200
Zhayo McCarter (7)	201
Rahma Abiona (7)	202
Isaac Curran-Leavy (8)	203
Thomas Lomax (8)	204
Amelia Harding Green (8)	205
Vanessa Vasilache (8)	206
Lucas Fieldhouse (7)	207
Marcie Watson (8)	208
Finley Dudley (7)	209
Ryan Ghorbani (7)	210
Felicity McGuirk (7)	211
Jack Davies (8)	212
Olivia Carroll-McArdle (8)	213
Charlotte Egan (7)	214
Scarlett Curran-Quinn (8)	215
Jessica Gledhill (7)	216
Benedict Nunn (7)	217
Maxwell Lindley (7)	218
Lottie Benson (7)	219
Dorcas Adebanjo (7)	220
Frankie Rowles (7)	221
Olivia Sloane (8)	222
Oliver Bates (8)	223
Charlie Hoyle (8)	224
Alayna Ansari (8)	225
Angus McGuire (7)	226

Poppie Rowles (7)	227
Temmy Edema (7)	228
Rosie Needham (7)	229
Annabelle Jupp (8)	230
Tiffany Burrows (7)	231
Aidan Starns (8)	232
Carl Orman (7)	233
Hebe Furtado Alves (7)	234

Ysgol Gymraeg Henllan, Henllan

Joseff Jackson (10)	235
Rhodri Cotterill (8)	236
Noa Evans (9)	238
Efa Parkes (9)	239
Erin Salusbury	240
Megan Davies (9)	241
Harvey Davies	242

THE POEMS

Nature's Blessing

Nature is sweet.
Nature gives you everything.
Nature's blessing.
Nature has butterflies.
Nature has bees.
Nature's blessing.
Nature has flowers.
Nature offers spring, autumn, summer and winter.
All of these are nature's blessings.
Be grateful for Mother Nature.
Nature provided you with land
In return can't you plant some trees?
Nature gives you blessings.
Just repay it by planting trees.

Siddique Mustafa (8)
Blair Peach Primary School, Southall

We Need Some Change Today

People are destroying Earth
What a lovely place it used to be!
We need to end this here and now
We need some sustainability!

We all need a change
So we can grow stronger
We can all do it
We need it more than ever

We need a way to end this
Right here, right now
Our chance to be heroes
Everyone around us needs to say wow

We can change the world
By picking up litter
Stop people from doing it
People hate litter

Recycling is great
For me and you
We are making a change
For the environment too

We all need to make a change
In the metrics
Even the cars
Are becoming electric.

Amber Ghai (9)
Blair Peach Primary School, Southall

Recharging Earth!

The Earth is our home, we must keep it bright,
With trees and flowers, shining in the light.
We must reduce, reuse, and recycle too,
To keep our planet, healthy and brand new.

Let's say goodbye to waste and hello to green,
With actions big and small, let's make a scene.
Together we can make a difference so large,
For an eco-friendly Earth, helping nature recharge!

Arnav Padam (8)
Blair Peach Primary School, Southall

A Leaf

A leaf is crisp and smooth.
A leaf is weird and funky.
A leaf is rolled up but fragrant.
A leaf is a great green but all rough.
A leaf's structure tells you a story.
A leaf is flying away to tell another living thing its story.
Leaves should be known because they tell a story of how Mother Nature created them.
Leaves are beautiful just like the rest of nature.

Eshal Luqman (9)
Blair Peach Primary School, Southall

Mini Prison

There are bars surrounding me everywhere,
Where do I go?
The only thing I can say is no!

What did I do wrong?
Why am I here?
But they just play ping-pong

While they are painting,
They keep me waiting,
Urgh, this is such a bore!
I wish I was near the shore.

Amanat Brar (9)
Blair Peach Primary School, Southall

Everything

Flowers are sweet
Lovely birds tweet
Trees so tall
People getting calls
Children jump
Porridge has lumps
Count up to ten
Chickens are in the pen
Sun so bright
Makes me feel so light
I feel heat
As the music beats
On the beach
I ate a peach.

Seryn Fenandes (8)
Blair Peach Primary School, Southall

Our Lovely Earth

Lovely Earth, lovely plants
But not so lovely anymore
Stop ruining our lovely Earth
Or we will suffer even more
So please stop doing that
Or you will get a slap
So hurry up and make your decision
Or you will have to do division.

Safia Mussa (8)
Blair Peach Primary School, Southall

Guess Who?

Blood lover
Plastic eater
Fast tail
Fish killer
Humans' nightmare
Human destroyer
Sharp teeth
Not many
Please don't litter in my habitat
Who am I?

Answer: I'm a shark.

Aathuja (9)
Blair Peach Primary School, Southall

Recycling

R ecycling, you may think it's good but sometimes people litter in the ocean and it kills too many animals.
E ven though it's hard to get out and about animals need our help like turtles, they get trapped in plastic and some die
C an you think of something you can do?
Y ou can change this so please help.
C an you think of something you can do right now to help?
L itter is horrible, especially for animals like turtles and fish, sharks and whales, who all get trapped.
I know you can help so can you please think of something?
N ow can you help today, please? If you can help, do
G reat things can be achieved so please help today.

Recycling can help the Earth.

Anna Vickers
Forest View Primary School, Whiteleas

Stop Littering

Our house is on fire.
Sharks are disappearing like magicians
But never coming back
Earth is crying
As tsunamis full of trash crash against the rocky shore.

Turtles are eating bags,
Animals are becoming extinct
Humans are polluting the air
The ocean is getting angrier every second.

Global warming everywhere
Mother Nature being destroyed
Piles of trash as tall as a mountain
Animals are desperate.

Stop cutting down nature's creations,
It's collapsing on top of them
Trees are falling like dominoes
There's less water to drink.

Clintin Vacher-Allan
Forest View Primary School, Whiteleas

Helping Nature

E mptying rubbish wherever they want
N ever pollute the oceans and rivers
V iolating our forests badly
I nvading animals' habitats, destroying their lives
R aising awareness is what we need to do
O ther people can help, we need to stick together
N ever contaminate, it's bad for everyone as
M ost animals need humans' help to survive
E ach and every one of us can play our part
N ow the animals can be safe and sound
T reat the environment with respect.

Noah Hall
Forest View Primary School, Whiteleas

The Environment

- **E** co-friendly, this is what we need to be
- **N** o more throwing away plastic please!
- **V** ery important lesson to be learnt.
- **I** mportant that you recycle, especially plastic.
- **R** ush to help the animals in the ocean
- **O** ceans of pollution are bad for our sea life
- **N** o more plastic in the ocean please
- **M** ean people are putting waste in the bin!
- **E** very person needs to play their part
- **N** o more plastic in the ocean please
- **T** heir habitats are not looking good.

Sophie Maxwell (9)
Forest View Primary School, Whiteleas

Saving Our Environment

E co-friendliness is vital to our survival
N ature green and growing
V oices caring for our Earth
I mportant solutions need to be heard
R ubbish discarded by human beings
O ceans are bulking up with rubbish and trash
N ever give up on saving the planet
M ake your habitat a friendly home
E very person can play the part
N ew life nowadays and new beginnings
T eamwork will make a better place to live for all of us.

Jack Day (8)
Forest View Primary School, Whiteleas

Help The Ocean

Plastic in the ocean
Turtles in prison growing unwell behind bars
Waves of plastic in the seas
Rubbish being eaten but not digested by animals.

The seas are crying for help
Plastic floating in the ocean like a deadly jellyfish
Stand up to the giants and tell them to stop littering, it's their only home

Animals crying and swimming around in the sea with all the plastic
They are getting hurt and their home is getting destroyed

Help the ocean.

Chloe Dunn
Forest View Primary School, Whiteleas

Save Our World

Stop chopping down Mother Nature's creations
Our poor animals are crying because we took their land
We are cutting down animals' homes
We need to stop destroying their habitats
The poor animals are helpless now
We took their land and ripped it apart

You could help by recycling and reusing rubbish
You can also help by picking up rubbish in all kinds of places
You have the power to save the animals
You have the power to save
Our environment.

Ayla Mayne (8)
Forest View Primary School, Whiteleas

Once And For All

Plastic bags are poisonous jellyfish,
Drifting along the polluted ocean,
Causing chaos and confusion,
To the unsuspecting fish.

Plastic ring pulls are giant pythons,
Strangling the undersea creatures,
Who can't hide in shallow nor deep water,
The deaths are multiplying.

But there is hope,
Piece by piece;
We save fish, whales and geese,
Plastic can be stopped.

We are powerful.
We can stop climate change;
Once and for all.

Once and for all.

Alex Smith (9)
Forest View Primary School, Whiteleas

Help The Oceans

The sea
Holds dozens of beautiful lives

Plastic bags pretend
To be jellyfish
For turtles to eat
Careless humans throwing their rubbish

A tsunami of plastic falls in the sea
The murky ocean cries for help
But nobody's listening
Nobody's here to hear their cries

What have humans done?

Bottles and bags
Get thrown in the sea by humans
Without a care in the world
Animals cry for help

What have humans done?

Amalie Cain
Forest View Primary School, Whiteleas

Recycling

R ubbish should never be thrown on the floor
E co-friendliness can help,
C an you help animals in the ocean?
Y ou should pick up rubbish when you see it on the floor,
C ans and paper can be recycled safely,
L et's work together to save the world,
I know that we can help
N ow our world will be nice and clean,
G ood luck in supporting the environment!

Daisy Fenwick
Forest View Primary School, Whiteleas

Let's Save The Planet

Humans corrupting the ocean with plastic
Have you seen what we've done?
Turtles imprisoned within our waste
Why is this happening?

Sea creatures feasting on garbage
Tangling in their stomach
Not getting digested
Why are we doing this?

Come on, let's work together
Let's start a war against littering
Our animals will be free and happy
We can achieve this goal

What are you waiting for?

Archie McGann (9)
Forest View Primary School, Whiteleas

Plastic In The Ocean

Plastic kills
You can help
You can recycle
You do not know where the plastic goes

If no bins are available, bring it home to put it in your bin
Poor turtles die because of pollution
Help our Mother Nature
The sea is more murky every day

Our world is at risk
From all of the littering
This is the only planet we have
Save our Mother Earth.

Ellis Cain (8)
Forest View Primary School, Whiteleas

Nature

The trees are like giants
The flowers are as tiny as an ant.
The bushes are sitting in the wind;
The trees are waving in the wind

Wildlife fear for their homes
Trash in the ocean
Making the sea murky
Killing animals

Our world is getting trashed
We need to help Mother Nature
Never give up on helping our Earth
We need to stop pollution.

Alfie Griffiths
Forest View Primary School, Whiteleas

Recycle

R ecycle, don't throw plastic in the ocean
E veryone can help by using less plastic
C an you please not throw plastic in the ocean?
Y ou can help by using fewer plastic bags too
C an you take care of Mother Earth?
L et's help the ocean by using less plastic
E veryone can do this.

Cory Speeding
Forest View Primary School, Whiteleas

Recycle

R euse plastic waste
E co-friendliness is very important
C ome and help animals struggling with plastic bottles
Y ou can help by cleaning oceans
C ome and make a massive difference to help sea creatures
L ittering can hurt animals
E co-friendliness will help Mother Nature.

Sydnie Corner (9)
Forest View Primary School, Whiteleas

Climate Change

Polar ice caps melting
Water rising
Causing floods and extreme weather
The planet is getting warmer

Plastic in the ocean
Killing and hurting marine wildlife
Plastic predator stalking its prey
Ready to attack
Turtle attacks the plastic and eats the bag
Humans can help by picking up trash from the ocean.

Joshua Conway
Forest View Primary School, Whiteleas

Save Animals' Homes

It's a disappointment when animals walk away
From their habitats
When the world is in humans' hands
Animals are homeless
It is pollution, trees and littering.

Have you looked at the trees?
Animals need them for their home
They are beautiful for the environment
Take care of the world around you.

Boux Sanderson (9)
Forest View Primary School, Whiteleas

Save Our Planet

Polar bears are getting hurt
The ice is melting away
Please stop burning fossil fuels
The weather is as loud, scary and angry as a bear

The weather is getting hotter
It's not good for the animals
The Antarctic is disappearing before our eyes
So animals are becoming extinct.

Ilayda Erol
Forest View Primary School, Whiteleas

Nature

N ow we should stop destroying forests
A nimals are homeless without woodland
T he forest is dying by human hands
U nder the leaves, the animals run for their lives
R educe, reuse and recycle
E very animal deserves to survive.

Summer Riley
Forest View Primary School, Whiteleas

Flower

F rozen flowers are very beautiful
L eaves fall from the big trees in winter
O wls make noises in the night
W inter is cold for the plants and for the animals
E verything is asleep in winter
R eady to plant in spring.

Lisa Krajewski
Forest View Primary School, Whiteleas

Save The Ocean!

Plastic is a tsunami in the waves
Crashing around
The polluted sea
Turtles eating plastic bags

Humans tossing plastic;
From left, right and centre;
From boats and cars
What have we done?

Logan Cooper
Forest View Primary School, Whiteleas

Forest Fires

There used to be a day when my branches stayed firmly
The leaves swayed in the wind
And I was safe.

But one day everything changed
A young man and his family left a campfire in the forest
The sun was too hot.
Slowly, everything burned.

Animals scuttled and scurried into the trees trying to get to safety
I felt scared as fire hurt my delicate leaves

But a few days later
The family who left the campfire came back
And helped rebuild the destroyed forest.
Flowers bloomed and trees grew.
Our forests always need a little bit of care!
Forests were green again and the family learned to save the forests
Because climate change matters!

Shannon Olusola-Johnson (11)
Hamilton College, Hamilton

Save The Planet

The hungry hunter chasing me down,
I hear sounds of trees falling to the ground,
A ton of plastic dumped on me,
A block of ice falling into the sea.

The ferocious fire crackling all around,
The giant blue whale ran aground,
Deadly gasses floating in the air,
Dangerous captors ill-treating the bear.

Temperatures rising sky-high everywhere,
Animal skins used as clothes for us to wear,
Oceans rising higher and higher every day,
The cat's owner abandoning it as a stray.

People wasting food by putting it in bins,
Nets in the ocean cutting dolphin and sharks' fins,
Car exhausts putting smoke in the air,
Animals saying it is not fair!

Electric cars being used more often,
People's hearts beginning to soften,
Trees being replanted everywhere,
Everyone doing their share.

Our planet is in need of help,
From elephants to the little kelp,
But there is a glimmer of hope in the future ahead,
We should not hurt our planet but help it instead.

Ethan Akun (10)
Hamilton College, Hamilton

Wasting World

Deafening sounds of fire fill panic in people's hearts,
Plastic floats through the ocean killing sea bass and carps,

My wonderful Earth is swallowed by puffing gas,
All for corrupt oil money getting spent fast,

But I can speak up and I have a voice,
To protest against all the noise,

Of desperate animals' cries telling people to stop,
All the extinct species and their tales made my bubble go *pop!*

I know speaking up against oil giants is bold,
But think of the icebergs that used to be cold!

All the polar bears suffering from the sun
And all the sounds of gunshots make animals run,

In Seattle, the residents were frightened by floods,
And protesters are dying, they're leaking blood,

Fills my heart with confident voices but also ferocious,
Telling me to speak up about all the warming oceans,

All the hurricanes and thunderstorms,
That make people run to their houses and dorms,

And Florida is more infested with tornadoes,
With hunters shooting antelopes like their foes,

And the lumberjacks fuel the fire,
Because cutting trees down is their desire,

And hurricanes blow people's lives away,
Like some pebbles or some hay,

And furred beasts are killed for fashion,
Their weak bodies come down crashing,

All may seem lost but we can make a change,
To rue the past and write on a new page,

With all of these problems unfurled,
We can change this wasting world!

Aryaman Reddy (10)
Hamilton College, Hamilton

The Great Tree

My friend the great tree sat proud and tall
Never thinking he would fall.
But in three short days
The birdie says
The man who holds a saw
Will come to withdraw
The finest sort of trees.
The tree thought, *oh no not me!*

Three days shortly passed,
The great tree was in a sort of fast.
He could not eat, drink or sleep
Knowing that the man with a saw
At his roots would gnaw.

Soon his time had come,
A tall man with leather boots stood in his path.
He said with a sharp tone
"I'm gonna cut this tree and take it home!"

As the not-so-great tree was loaded up
The birdie came with utter shock

"Who will dance with the wind now that you're gone?
Who will keep me safe on a cold winter morn?"

The tree could simply not reply,
He just knew that he would die.
The birdie almost started to cry
"Why oh why this great-great tree?
He's been here for centuries just sitting with me."

The man with a saw started his car,
The whole forest shook then off he went.
The birdie tried to ask the man to repent
But the birdie could not catch up
And so waited and waited trying to cheer up.

After a while another bird dropped by,
"Why oh why must you cry?"
The birdie sighed, "That tree was my home."
Then the other bird left him to roam.

Now that is it, my good friend,
Maybe not all stories have a happy end.

Rebecca Coughlan (10)
Hamilton College, Hamilton

A Honeybee And A Honey Bear

The honeybee and the honey bear
Who live in the forest seem to be an odd pair
Though they share honey and care
For everything there.

When the bee is in the hive,
The bear is in the cave feeling alive
But then he tried to get to sleep and he tried and he tried,
The bear said, "It's too hot for sleep but it's the middle of autumn and it should be in a freeze."
Then he sat on a log next to the river whilst sipping his honey next to the bees
He suddenly shouted, "What's that in the trees?"

He heard a chop then another and another
Until he heard someone shout, "Take cover!"
He then looked around and heard a thud,
Just before he was about to hide in the mud.

He ran over as fast as he could
Until he had seen a big lump of wood
There was a man behind it
Then he looked over the river and saw cans all over it,
"What has happened to the lush forest?
At this rate it will become a bush with no trees."
The bear searched for a way to stop it
Until there was a police officer who said, "Halt it!"

The bees and the bear couldn't believe their eyes
There were protests trying to save the world,
Later the forest was finally free
At last now the bear can finally relax.

Benjamin Psaila (10)
Hamilton College, Hamilton

Red Panda - My Journey To Extinction

I am just a red panda, could I be the last?
My family were gone really fast.

Someone save our species,
We are going extinct.

The last words my family said were "I love you,
Your sister should take care of you."

But we are just two
It's me and you.

They have gone to rest
I have done my best.

But there are hunters who want our fur.
I cannot stop thinking about the future.

My sister has a baby on the way.
Her husband has gone to look for a safe place.

My sister and I are sad
But we cannot turn back.

I don't want this life for the baby on the way.
My sister's husband got us a new place today.

There is a long journey to be done.
But this one is not going to be fun.

We have to go fast
But again, what about the past?

There was a lot of running.
A wildfire was burning.

There are fewer of us now,
Than at the start of our journey.

Oreoluwa Akinkugbe (10)
Hamilton College, Hamilton

Saving The Planet

We could change the world,
Oh yes we could,
If everyone everywhere does as they should.

Walking to your destination,
Might just solve a big situation!

If leaders take charge the problem will be solved,
But fighting and arguing will not help at all.

There is no planet two,
But there is a lot we can do.

Our planet has been here for us,
Through highs and lows.

Our colossal planet is heating up,
We need to take a stand before time is up.

As we take charge things will change,
For the choice between peace or destruction lies in your hands.

Will you change the world for better or worse?

Bella Babalola (10)
Hamilton College, Hamilton

The Climate Impact On Ocean Life

As the ocean ebbs and flows, the rising water levels begin to grow.

Lots of plastic floating by, makes many animals want to cry,
Because some of their friends begin to die,
As more and more pollution is added to our waters.

Climate change is real!
Our planet is becoming warmer.
We need to become an informer,
And spread the word about how to become a performer
In helping save the environment for ourselves and the wildlife.

There are lots of ways to help.
Don't be rash, recycle your trash!
Help save our beautiful seas and sea life for future generations.
If we don't, sadly some species may become extinct.

Flynn Thomson (10)
Hamilton College, Hamilton

Rubbish In The Sea

R ubbish is not for me
U nder the sea
B in bags full of plastic
B alloons and elastic
I s waiting to kill the fish
S alty and clean, I wish
H ow can this be achieved?

I n the sea, so much debris
N ot for me

T he sea is not for waste
H umpback whales should not be faced, with
E ndless amounts of litter to taste

S ee the garbage all gathered up
E els getting tangled up!
A nd all because of humans.

Rafe Chesworth (10)
Hamilton College, Hamilton

I Am Your Earth

I am your Earth
I am your home
But you destroy
My skin and bone

But I forgive
And I forget
I let you live
But I regret.

Do you realise
I'm your only hope?
So don't stand around and mope
I need saving
And it's up to you
This is what I need you to do

No more plastic
No more waste
Because I am fading at a fast pace
I need love
And I need care
Because you are puffing and panting my air.

Jorja Smith (10)
Hamilton College, Hamilton

Save The Fish

S cared fish swimming around the ocean
A quatic animals dying every day
V iolent, rude plastic ruling the ocean
E xtremely large animals in the sea are eating the wrong food

T errible acts of fly-tipping
H orrible waste in the ocean
E veryone thinks it's okay to kill the sea

F inally fish are being saved
I n the sea everyone once swam in
S ad fish swim in the ocean now
H elp the fish be happy!

Blyth Robertson (10)
Hamilton College, Hamilton

Earth And Fire

E arth is an endangered place.
A nimals are dying.
R hinos are becoming extinct.
T he Earth is becoming polluted.
H igh water levels rising.

A nimal habitats going extinct.
N ature is dying.
D rought is happening.

F orest fires are happening.
I cebergs are melting.
R econstruction has to happen because of the fires.
E arthquakes are evolving.

Tafara Mutezo (10)
Hamilton College, Hamilton

The River Ness

R ushing and gushing from the melting snow.
I ngenious humans harness the flow.
V eering around obstacles as you go.
E co-friendly power generation.
R unning homes and factories as you fall.

N ever-ending supply of water flows through the turbine.
E lectricity generated with every turn.
S upplying green energy for the local community.
S wimmers kept warm by the endless flow.

Max Boyd (10)
Hamilton College, Hamilton

The Clear Water

The water as still as death.
Calm, still and clear as can be.

Clouds gather over the water but the water is not clear anymore.
Rain pours down, you hear thunder in the mere distance.
Waves strike the shore.

Lightning crashes down to the dark black water.
The wind starts crying out.
Waves smash against each other 'til the sun shines down.

The clouds clear and the water is as clear as can be.

Blair Kinnoch (10)
Hamilton College, Hamilton

Endangered Animals

E lephants and so many other animals slowly fading away.
N ot being helped.
D eath and danger all around them.
A nimals being killed for our own good.
N owhere to go.
G oods and foods just being wiped away.
E xtinct a couple of years later.
R ights for animals being ignored.
E ffort put in for no reason.
D eadly things surround them.

Kathleen Bullen (10)
Hamilton College, Hamilton

Stormy Seas

Waves as soft as a gliding dove,
The dolphins singing full of love.
Waves splashing against the bay.
The fish coming out to play.

The waves begin to crash, the water roars,
Fear all throughout all the animals' cores.
But don't forget one small, important thing,
The killer whale will always be the king!

Caleb Browning (10)
Hamilton College, Hamilton

A Leaf Of A Lifetime

The leaf zigzagged to the ground
Will it ever be found?
It felt the wind swirling around
As it zigzagged to the ground.

The leaf landed in the sea
How can I save the Earth, what is the key?
What is this horrid plastic in the sea?
Humans can be cruel, how can this be?

Isaac Jalil (10)
Hamilton College, Hamilton

The Earth Is Dying!

The Earth is dying from the trees on fire,
The flames are red and yellow.
Before the fire, the tall trees were brown.
When the trees are on fire, they turn to black and white ashes,
The fires are very hot like lava.

I can smell burning wood and I can hear breaking sounds,
I think it's very hot.

The flames are killing the animals,
Their homes are being destroyed.
The fire is as red as strawberries.
The smoke is grey and it hurts my eyes.
It smells.

The Earth is dying!
We should change this because it's bad for the environment.

Logan Barter (11)
Lakeside School, Chandler's Ford

Global Warming...

Global warming is a problem and plastic isn't helping!
The sea has more plastic than ten recycle bins.
Fish are getting stuck in the plastic.
We need to recycle more!

Global warming can be a challenge!
All the wildfires are very bad.
It's burning down Australia and animals are dying.
We need to look after the Earth!

Global warming needs to stop!
The ice is melting and polar bears are suffering.
The water is rising rapidly and land is flooding.
We need to change our ways!

Archie Greaves (10)
Lakeside School, Chandler's Ford

Squirrels

Squirrels are small and cute.
They live in trees, in nests called dreys.

Squirrels can be red or grey.
Their lifespan is five to ten years.

Squirrels like to eat nuts and seeds.
They hold their food between their paws.

Squirrels' large ears help them pick up the quietest sounds.
Their bushy tails twitch to send signals to other squirrels and help them balance.

I think squirrels are cute.
We should look after them.

Koby Bartlett (11)
Lakeside School, Chandler's Ford

Dreams Of A Better World...

When you cut down a tree, plant five more in its place.
Recycle all plastics and glass.
No open fires in burnable places.
No smoking - it's bad for you.
No littering.
Use renewable energy.
Stop climate change.
No pollution.
Protect the environment.
Live in harmony!

Dexter Wyeth Whitfield (11)
Lakeside School, Chandler's Ford

Wildfire

W ildlife is on fire,
I nsects are in danger,
L eopards are leaving,
D eadly deforestation,
F ood is burning,
I nside is scorching hot,
R ed ferocious flames,
E ndangering life.

Leon Cawley (10)
Lakeside School, Chandler's Ford

The Ocean

I am the ocean, I need you to save me
Plastic swims through me, which makes me cry
I ask all the plastic why it's here
It just says, "Humans don't recycle me
I have nowhere else to live!"
So humans!
Humans!
Recycle! Recycle!
You're hurting me!
All the animals are getting hurt!
From whale sharks to turtles to tiny little fish
Remember they live here too!
So humans!
Humans!
Recycle! Recycle!
Remember we live here too!

Halimah Hussain (10)
St Margaret's CE Primary School, Great Barr

Planet Poem

O ur planet
U nique in every way
R ecycle and reuse

P ollution sadness
L ife-giver
A ctivity maker
N ature all around
E nvironment needs help
T rees and forests dying.

Harlem Hendra-Smith (10)
St Margaret's CE Primary School, Great Barr

The Amazing Earth!

W e live on it, we breathe it and we love it
O ur home
R espect Earth
L ove our Earth
D elightful Earth

We should save our Earth
Our beautiful planet Earth

Our home
Where our friends and family live
Where it is land and sea
Life-giver
We all have a part to play
Where nature is

We should save our Earth
Our beautiful planet Earth.

Sarah Kouevi (10)
St Margaret's CE Primary School, Great Barr

Deforestation

D anger to the planet
E ndangered animals
F orest fires
O ne and all must make a change
R emember to recycle
E veryone is a team to protect this planet
S ave our planet
T hreats to the environment
A nimals are dying
T rees are being chopped down
I t is time to change
O ur responsibility
N ature is fading away.

Jiya Jagpal (9)
St Margaret's CE Primary School, Great Barr

Pollution

P ollution is killing our planet Earth
O ceans are full of it
L ike the world we do not want
L itter needs to stop now
U nwanted sea litter needs to go away
T oday this will stop
I t is our duty to stop this
O ur Earth is at risk
N ow is our time to step up and go

Say no to pollution
Say yes to a new world.

Isabelle Shakespeare (9)
St Margaret's CE Primary School, Great Barr

What Is Happening?

O ur planet was beautiful,
U ntil we destroyed it,
R eally, we are destroying it.

P lants and trees are being killed,
L ife on Earth is soon to be a legend,
A nimals are going extinct,
N atural wildlife is becoming less and less,
E very living thing is disappearing,
T ime for us to stop this.

Ariyanna Turner-Rathbone (10)
St Margaret's CE Primary School, Great Barr

Endangered Animals

Endangered animals need help
They are critically endangered
We are losing them
They are going extinct
Which is not very good
What would we do without them?
They are being hunted
Endangered, endangered
Oh what can we do?
We all need to remember the planet is theirs as well
Remember, remember.

Eliza Flora (10)
St Margaret's CE Primary School, Great Barr

Our Planet!

O utstanding beauty
U nique in every way
R ecycling is important

P rotect nature
L emons, fruit and vegetables
A ctive, ready to protect nature
N ature is a wonderful thing
E arth's environment needs to be saved
T rees and rainforests fading away.

Jovan Jagpal (9)
St Margaret's CE Primary School, Great Barr

What Am I?

I'm being polluted
You're killing my animals
You can go through me
You can discover my depths
I'm transparent
Although I seem blue
I move with the moon
Recycle to save me
You may see yourself as a reflection
What am I?

Answer: The ocean.

Dhiren Flora (9)
St Margaret's CE Primary School, Great Barr

What Am I?

Deep swimmer
A talented fighter
Tentacle swisher
Ten legs and a colossal giant
What am I?

Answer: A squid.

Huge biter
Deep ocean swimmer
King fight taker
Food scavenger
What am I?

Answer: A shark.

Finley Mcdonald (10)
St Margaret's CE Primary School, Great Barr

Our World

O utstanding beauty
U nique collection of habitats
R oom for all species

W e all have a responsibility
O ur future depends on it!
R educe, reuse and recycle
L ove the planet we have been given
D o it now!

Skye Clarke (10)
St Margaret's CE Primary School, Great Barr

Litter

L itter is bad for the environment
I t is time to change
T ime to stop leaving litter on the floor
T ime to change from plastic bags
E veryone must change
R eally need to stop this!

Matilda Johnson (9)
St Margaret's CE Primary School, Great Barr

Pacific

P oseidon's here
A clear great place
C lownfish roam the sea
I nfected with litter
F amous for its seascapes
I n the world emerged
C rabs might be at the bottom.

Arvind Singh Bains (10)
St Margaret's CE Primary School, Great Barr

Forest

Flowers blooming
Birds singing
Branches swaying
Wind wailing
Leaves crunching
Squirrels climbing
Mud slushing
Seasons changing
Water trickling.

Harley Morris (9)
St Margaret's CE Primary School, Great Barr

Ocean

O utstanding beauty
C oral reefs
E lectricity provider
A ctivities such as surfing or sailing
N ot in our future because plastic is choking it!

Amirah Shaikh (9)
St Margaret's CE Primary School, Great Barr

Earth

Life giver
Litter keeper
Habitat provider
Gravity guardian
Food grower
Diverse species

Please help save our beautiful planet!

Alfie Fowler (9)
St Margaret's CE Primary School, Great Barr

Panda

A kennings poem

Bamboo chomper
Tree climber
Big eater
Serial sleeper
Striped walker
Green nature
Central China
Playful player.

Katie Shaw (10)
St Margaret's CE Primary School, Great Barr

Our Planet
A kennings poem

Life giver
Gravity holder
Litter keeper
Food grower
Habitat provider
Flower maker

Home for all.

William Pedley (9)
St Margaret's CE Primary School, Great Barr

The Earth

A kennings poem

Life giver
Litter keeper
Habitat giver
Land protector
Food provider
Gravity guardian
Home for all.

Olivia Bell (9)
St Margaret's CE Primary School, Great Barr

Save Our Earth!

Pondering on the disasters and misery around you
Do you think this is not because of you?
The sorrowful and dull environment,
Does this not need your love and empowerment?
Have you explored what's the matter?
Have you tried climbing up the reasoning ladder?
Climb up, climb up and please see
It won't cost you a dime, it is absolutely free!

The tired animals are going extinct
As we speak, and each time you blink,
Give it a helping hand when it needs it the most
Earth is crying, Earth is dying
Save our planet, save our Earth!

Musa Ghalib (10)
Suffah Primary School, Hounslow

A Majestic Summer Day

The winter breeze is away
That means it is summer
The majestic animals start emerging
Birds tweeting
What a beautiful summer day

The deer hear creaking
The trees sway
But why is it not a majestic summer day?

As strangers enter
They destroy nature
But why do they have to be horrible?
Thousands of trees get cut down
Everybody, it's time for action

To stop the trees getting cut down
We must stand together
The weather is changing
Leaves falling

But why
Isn't it summer?
Well it might be because of biodiversity
Fewer animals and more humans

Everybody let's stand together
Help nature
From those treacherous strangers

Please stop this nonsense
Instead be joyful
Help the animals and surrender!

Yasirah Aaidah (10)
Suffah Primary School, Hounslow

The Heartless Massacre

The spring breeze relieves its lungs
The bears wake up to the birds' songs,
The first flowers awake to see
Flying ashes and burning trees

The mechanical monsters clearing the way
To bring biodiversity to its horrendous dismay
The giant creatures chop our trees
Without guilt or regret, we see

We shall come with our revenge
For this heartless massacre
All for something else that is named money
Them laughing as if our suffering is funny

The destroying machineries do not see
They shall meet a devastating death when we leave

The heartless massacre
Shall occur again
Leaving them and their offspring breathless
With the money in their pockets that would be truly useless.

Syeda Aliya Ahmad-Shah (11)
Suffah Primary School, Hounslow

What Is Nature?

As is the way the glowing stars go,
As is the way the peaceful wind will blow.
As you see time come and go,
The same way you see someone from a young age,
and then grow.

Like paint, red, yellow and blue,
You will know that nature has colours too.
Violet, green, indigo and maroon,
Nature is even a part of even dusk and noon.

Nature is why time runs,
And once time begins, it never turns.
Some people find life boring, some find it fun
But remember your life will end soon after it has begun.

So remember that nature is amazing,
But you should also remember to take care of it while you're living.

Muhammad Bashir (11)
Suffah Primary School, Hounslow

There's No Time To Waste!

The forest needs us
This is a must
The trees are calling
They know the birds are stalling

Out in the wild
No one remembers when they smiled
They look at each other
For they have not so long lives to suffer

The howling and angry wind, that was once a breeze,
Doesn't whisper anymore, just makes the branches freeze
The white sheets of snow accompanying me every year,
Now it is never coming anywhere near

What is happening with our Earth, our home, our trees?
It is painful to watch the extinction of our happy bees

Come sit with me and learn this for once,
Nature is our hope,
It's time to put the cruelty against the Earth to stop!

Asma Mohamed (11)
Suffah Primary School, Hounslow

Take A Chance And Go Outside

Whenever you go outside you enjoy your time.
You feel relieved and have no stress on your mind.
All that surrounds you is nature filled with peace.
You can hear birds tweeting from different trees.
Peace is all a person needs.
How do you think Isaac Newton discovered gravity?
He enjoyed his time and finally found peace.
So even one theory can prove that if you go outside you enjoy your time.
Ideas really do come to your mind.
So if you really want peace just go outside.
Lots of animals may surround you but they really aren't here to harm you.
So go outside and enjoy your time.

Muna Abdelrahman (11)
Suffah Primary School, Hounslow

Nature

Nature is for all
The leaves begin to fall
Calling trees
Honey is made by bees
Barking dogs
Children play in the park
Soon the sun sets
It becomes dark
The next bright day
Another awesome month of May
Chirping birds, saying tweet tweet
Come outside to see nature!

Zaybah Sultan (11)
Suffah Primary School, Hounslow

Plants Are So Beautiful

The plants are so beautiful
And so loveable
And some plants are untouchable
Just go outside it is enjoyable
It is not avoidable
Just go outside and sit down and enjoy the view.

Jamal Takar (11)
Suffah Primary School, Hounslow

My Beautiful, Brilliant, Beloved World

The tweets as birds fly across the sky,
The smell of newly cut grass seeping through the air,
The feel of the snow melting in your hand,
The rushing waterfall as it tumbles over the rocks,
My beautiful, brilliant, beloved world.

The booming waves echoing through the air,
The deafening roar of the thundering waves,
The itchy feeling of the grass as you lie in the meadow,
The muddy, drippy, watery mud dripping off your shoe,
My beautiful, brilliant, beloved world.

The dripping blue rain pouring down my coat,
The icy chill of the snow gently nestling on my face,
The fresh smell of spring and summer,
Outside, a tall crowd of large green trees.
My beautiful, brilliant, beloved world.

Elizabeth Johnson (11)
Windermere Preparatory School, Windermere

My Stunning, Unique, Yet Suffering World

Thousands of little critters floating around aimlessly,
Pond skaters racing around the pond,
A little ecosystem is simply thriving in their little pocket of the Earth,
Little tadpoles growing by the hour,
Kingfishers dive into the water looking for lunch,
Towering reeds peek out the water like submarine periscopes,
Frogs jump in and out of the water,
But it's not all perfect,
The ponds are drying out faster than ever,
Wonderful species die out,
My stunning, unique, yet suffering world.

Towering mountains glisten in the morning sun,
Mountain goats cling onto the smallest of holes,
The clouds settle over us like a freezing blanket of coldness,
Eagles soar over the mountains looking for their prey,

The smallest of animals somehow survive in this harsh, punishing land,
But it's not all perfect,
The snow is melting faster than ever,
Glaciers which have been building for millions of years are melting away,
My stunning, unique, yet suffering world.

The ghostly blanket of dark gloomy clouds approach, signalling a storm,
Little critters and big mammals alike take refuge in the caves,
The splish-splosh of the water falling to the ground,
The stalagmites and stalactites reaching for each other,
As you look on to the jet-black abyss of darkness,
Creatures who have never seen sunlight take refuge here,
But it's not all perfect,
The caves may get filled with water,
Humans mine out this stunning area of the world,
My stunning, unique, yet suffering world.

George Allen (11)
Windermere Preparatory School, Windermere

My Majestic, Marvellous, Mystical World

The gentle breeze fills my lungs with joy, happiness,
and a newfound sense of confidence,
The green, green grass glistens under the blue,
blue sky,
As I walk outside on a warm spring day,
I see the birds singing their beautiful, brilliant song,
When I walk outside on a chilly winter day,
I hear the crunch and crisp of the frozen grass
beneath my warm winter boots,
Minute fish hop around the pond as the people
gaze at them in awe,
The stunning bath of water shimmers and glistens
under the scorching sun on a boiling summer day.
My majestic, marvellous, mystical world.

Wild, overgrown plants swarm the empty spaces of
land,
The glistening sun gazes down at the beautiful
land like a big bright light bulb,
The moon looks down on us like a humongous
night light,

The smell of a fresh new day as you walk outside on a warm summer morning,
The massive, beautiful trees sway magically under the magical orange sunset,
The wonderful ice-capped mountains almost shave the stars,
Majestic birds soar through the sky looking over us all.
My majestic, marvellous, mystical world.

You can taste the bitter smoke fill your lungs with unpleasantness,
The beautiful adjacent air makes you feel amazing,
The jet-black abyss of darkness at nighttime,
The sheep devour the green grass calmly and peacefully.
My majestic, marvellous, mystical world.

Jonah Lewis
Windermere Preparatory School, Windermere

My Magical, Mystical, Yet Perishing Home

My home is dying: though they say they try everything, they don't,
The ash clouds are irrelevant even though they won't go away, they wouldn't with climate change,
I want climate change to go away because then we would live a perfect life,
My dream planet is without fossil fuels and coal mines,
I want a planet without cutting down those hundreds of trees a day,
I want a life without people making money in a business that makes coal in a coal mine.

I want to live without making money by doing harmful stuff to the environment,
I want to live without ash clouds in the greying sky,
I want to live with just a cyanic sky and not ash clouds,
I want to live a more sustainable life,

I want to live without factories making smoke,
I want to live without trees being cut down,

My dream life is with solar panels,
My life is with fuel.

Louis Bromley (11)
Windermere Preparatory School, Windermere

Our Beautiful World

Never-ending fields go on forever,
Trees blowing in the wind magically,
Wind blowing loudly so much you can hear it,
Soft grass so soft you can sleep on it,
Colourful flowers coming through,
Our beautiful world.

The sun shining so bright you cannot look at it,
The sunset so beautiful,
The cows mooing loudly you can hear them from a mile away,
The sun so hot it burns,
The flowers' bright colours glistening in the light,
Our beautiful world.

The trees quickly losing their bright orange leaves,
Walking on the crisp orange leaves,
All the trees are now bare,
The clouds are towering over us,
Muddy puddles everywhere,
Our beautiful world.

The bitter wind blowing in our faces,
Towering snow-capped mountains,
The ground is hard in places,
Snow all around,
Crisp white under foot,
Our beautiful world.

Oliver Gale (11)
Windermere Preparatory School, Windermere

My Magical, Beloved, Stunning Planet

The frosty, crunchy, crispy air flowing through my mouth,
The feel of the powdery air flashing against my face,
The bitter smoke filling my lungs,
The howling wind whistling in my ear,
Brilliant green grass fluttering in my eyes,
My magical, beloved, stunning planet.

The rushing waterfall tumbling over the grey rocks,
White clouds arguing in the sky,
The taste of the crunchy snow,
The soft crawling coldness crawling down my spine,
Muddy, drippy, watery mud squelching off my shoe,
My magical, beloved, stunning planet.

The cold blue water freshly falling off the clouds,
The taste of fresh morning dew,
The dripping blue rain falling off the crispy leaves,

The minty taste of the flowing stream,
The feel of the waves bashing on your feet,
My magical, beloved, stunning planet.

Eve Wearmouth (11)
Windermere Preparatory School, Windermere

My Beautiful, Amazing, Stunning Environment

The tough, steep mountains waiting to be climbed,
The bracing aroma of the newly grown mint leaves,
The astonishing wonders of my back garden,
waiting to be discovered,
The birds soaring gracefully in the royal-blue sky,
The crisp, refreshing air seeping into my lungs,
The unignorable itch of the green grass resting on my face.
My beautiful, amazing, stunning environment.

The crashing of the gushing waves creeping up my spine,
The sweet, crunchy apple hovering over my mouth,
The creepy-crawlies scurrying in and out of their habitats,
The bright blue sky with the cotton candy clouds,
The animals returning to their natural habitats
after a long day of hunting.
My beautiful, amazing, stunning environment.

Harry Owens (11)
Windermere Preparatory School, Windermere

My Marvellous, Magical, Mystical World

The dripping rain blue rain splashing on the puddles,
The breath-taking mist against your face in the morning,
The taste of the harsh blizzard in the thick air,
The feeling of frostbite from the cold bite in the air,
My marvellous, magical, mystical world.

The sound of cows having a quick catnap,
The feel of the emptiness in the air,
The feel of the harsh weather on my face,
The leaves plummeting down off the statuesque trees,
My marvellous, magical, mystical world.

Verity Larkins (11)
Windermere Preparatory School, Windermere

My Wonderful, Winsome, But Unhappy World

The blooming flowers in the wind,
Oh the wind, the noisy deafening wind,
The trees rustle in it,
The smell of the seaside - icy and salty,
The feeling of when you cannot do anything after a storm,
The soft sand that happens after the hot warm sand,
The taste of the morning dew,
My wonderful, winsome, but unhappy world.

Natalee Rowe
Windermere Preparatory School, Windermere

My Amazing, Magical, Yet Endangered World

Amazing plants and trees growing by the days,
The high, deadly, pointy mountains,
The beautiful view of the summer sun,
I wish,
I wish we all could live in a better world without bad things,
I want to live in a world
In a beautiful world.

Vincent Koenig (10)
Windermere Preparatory School, Windermere

Save The World

In the trees are bees on their knees
Begging please.
Why just stand there
And watch the world crumble in despair?
It is a crime
If you don't save the animals you're running out of time.

The turtles are in danger
Save them before it becomes fatal
All the animals that you see today
They're not going to play
Tomorrow there will be sorrow.
The water won't pour
All the animals will fall on the floor
The sea won't flow
All the animals will go.
My heart breaks
As the trees shake
And we take the animals' souls away

The animals are dying because our nation is
cutting down our trees
So please
Make a change to the world.

Leo Robinson (10) & Maja Grodzka (11)
Woodland Community Primary School, Heywood

The World Flashes Before Its Eyes

Frustration, deforestation, chopping down trees brings despair everywhere.
Extinction is very close, all the animals you know and love will go.
Year 2050 all animals are gone, pandas, gorillas, they're gone
Solution is don't chop down trees
The only reason you're doing it is because you're mean.
Sea levels rising every time
All the ice caps melting, people say 'it's fine'
But they're wrong, the solution to stop climate change
It's not that hard, it's not a pain.
Littering, all lights on, driving, not even recycling
Solution: no littering, all lights off and recycling, that's the way
Now animals will live another day.

Mylo Ferns (10)
Woodland Community Primary School, Heywood

Why Do We Do This?

I'll break your knees if you kill the bees that live in the trees,
Because at the end of the day the sky will fade away,
Do we really need long showers instead of flowers?
You'll try to smile but it won't last a while
We need to make a change, are we on the same page?

The sky is dying, polar bears are crying,
The fish will die, there will be no sky
The birds won't fly and everyone will cry
Floods will cover the sky, do you really want this?
Well I think we should make a change
Go different ways
Eat less meat
And maybe just maybe we might not feel defeat
And by writing this it should inspire others to listen!

Jaydan Clegg (11)
Woodland Community Primary School, Heywood

I Remember When...

I remember when...
The ocean was a paradise to us all
However the living nightmare came and destroyed all of our glory.
I remember when...
The animals in the ocean had tsunamis of happiness
However the devil in disguise came and ripped the ocean heart apart which destroyed 75% of the world.
I remember when...
The ocean felt like heaven however the devil made a nightmare of the ocean and now the ocean feels like hell.
I remember when...
The sea was the heart of the Earth and billions came
However the murderer came along and broke the life of the ocean apart.

Athanasios Karanikas (10)
Woodland Community Primary School, Heywood

Save The World

I can't believe it's finally time,
To write a poem about this crime,
Things you did to the animals,
Are not quite understandable.

Animals are dying,
Birds are flying,
Flying in the air,
The air that you didn't give a care!

As time goes by ice caps are melting,
And all you care about is your wealth.
Polar bears have felt,
Like their homes have had a bad deal and it's all your fault

So we need to think fast,
So that our animals will last,
If we work together,
It will be with us forever,
So quickly do your bit,
You won't regret it...

Lacie Keefe (11)
Woodland Community Primary School, Heywood

I Remember When...

I remember when...
The ocean was a sea of dreams,
However, the animal killer came along and killed the animals in its path.

I remember when...
The salty sea was the heart of Earth,
However, the devil in disguise crept along and floated along on its surface.

I remember when...
The crystal-clear sea was a bubble of tranquillity,
However, the floating demon came and took the tsunami of happiness.

I remember when...
The sea was a beauty of water,
However, the king of devils came and ruined the ocean.

Isla Ashton (9)
Woodland Community Primary School, Heywood

I Remember When...

I remember when...
The sea was like the key to paradise.
However, the devil of the land made a tsunami filled with anger.

I remember when...
The sea was the most liked place ever.
Although, an unknown visitor entered the sea, killing fish.

I remember when...
The ocean was a paradise for all.
Until suddenly, a devil ripped all the beauty out of it.

I remember when...
Animals lived in peace.
Until a tsunami of all kinds attacked the sea of dreams scaring off the fish.

Madison Matthews (9)
Woodland Community Primary School, Heywood

I Remember When

I remember when...
The ocean was a perfect fantasy,
However, a murderer ripped out its soul.

I remember when...
The animals floated in waves of happiness,
However, they got wiped out and now float alongside devils in disguise.

I remember when...
It was paradise,
However, a poison bomb released and chaos began.

I remember when...
The heart of the Earth was a full-pieced puzzle,
However, the killer's hook smashed it into pieces.

Matylda Knach (10)
Woodland Community Primary School, Heywood

Save The World

Deforestation, racism, our world has gone to the tip,
One day our world will rip.
One day you will sit crying,
Wondering why all of these animals are dying.
Your future kids
Will never be able to experience the things that you did.
The animals that you adore will be dying on the floor,
Whimpering and crying, you could open a new door.
You love your designer coat and that leopard loved its mother,
Unlike the leopard you can buy another,
But that leopard cannot buy another mother.

Logan Done
Woodland Community Primary School, Heywood

I Remember When...

I remember when...
The oceans were filled with many species,
Until one day,
That was the worst day in history.

I remember when...
The oceans had tsunamis of pure happiness,
But the demon froze those tsunamis of happiness.

I remember when...
The ocean was like heaven on Earth,
But the devil arrived and demolished everything that was happy.

I remember when...
Every single fish in the sea was happy like the sun,
The demon came and turned those smiles upside down.

Dominik Stankowski (10)
Woodland Community Primary School, Heywood

I Remember When...

I remember when...
The sea was the heart of the Earth
But however, came a tsunami of a different kind.

I remember when...
The ocean was a paradise for all
However, the devil of the Earth came and created hell on Earth.

I remember when...
The ocean was a safe haven like a rainbow
But, however, a murderer came and made a living nightmare.

I remember when...
The ocean had a tsunami of happiness
However, the king of devils came and destroyed the tsunami in its tracks.

Charlie Lees (9)
Woodland Community Primary School, Heywood

I Remember When...

I remember when...
The water was clean with no plastic.
Life was a tsunami of happiness and life was fun playing with the animals.

I remember when...
There were no animals dying every day for years.
The days were happy, it was breathtaking.

I remember when...
The days were easier.
It is barely memorable now.

The plastic is destroying the Earth, murdering animals, strangling innocent dolphins and choking cute turtles.
This is like hell in the sea.

Archie Green (9)
Woodland Community Primary School, Heywood

The Rainforest

T he rainforest is a place for animals.
H arm them, they'll die.
E veryone has to stop littering!

R ain falls on trees.
A ir is what animals breathe in.
I n rainforests, there's trees and plants.
N o killing animals!
F orests are unique!
O ur planet needs help!
R estore the planet.
E at other food, not animals!
S tore food for us!
T ake care of the planet.

Jemima Lokongo (8)
Woodland Community Primary School, Heywood

Protect Our World

Plastic on the floor,
Wind knocking on the door,
Our land is now poor,
For protection we need more,

Trees are falling,
Animals are crying,
What are we thinking?
Our planet is sinking!

Plastic is strangling our innocent animals,
All of them are crying,
Mother Nature is dying,

Smoke and gas ravage our air,
Stealing our oxygen,
People cannot bear.

No hope to be found,
Help is needed now,
Plastic is hurting our world,

We need to protect our Earth.

Lola Barlow (9)
Woodland Community Primary School, Heywood

Rainforest

R aindrops hitting the ground
A round are a lot of animals who see their trees get cut down
I s it even safe for them?
N obody even dared to save the trees
F or they are afraid of what they see
O f course the toucans fled
R esting koalas and sloths were waking up
E verybody was waking up
S o many animals were hiccupping in shock
T he monkeys swung away. Tick-tock, please stop.

Harley Burgess (9)
Woodland Community Primary School, Heywood

I Remember When...

I remember when...
The ocean was the sea of dreams full of peace,
However, the devil came from nowhere and started murdering animals.
I remember when...
The ocean was like a safe bubble,
However, then started nightmare and chaos.
I remember when...
It was beauty in the ocean,
However, the devil was even in the water.
I remember when the ocean was like a rainbow,
However, the devil was in the disguise.

Egor Konyshev (9)
Woodland Community Primary School, Heywood

Helping Earth

H elp the Earth, it is in danger
E arth is in a terrible environment.
L ife is fading away.
P eople are littering.
I t's time to take action.
N o one is using the bins.
G iraffes are endangered, help.

E arth is a living hell.
A rctic is melting slowly but surely.
R eally! Listen to the news.
T he Earth needs help now.
H elp the environment.

Jacob Sutton
Woodland Community Primary School, Heywood

Save The Planet

Sorry we left you with all our mess
The planet's population is here less and less.
You're changing and harming our precious
Planet day by day,
By staining it with pollution even still today.

Animals want to live and birds want to fly
But you won't let it happen because of all the gas in the sky.
The clouds go white to black full with steam
Made of poisonous gas that flows down the river and streams.

Lillie Sigsworth (11)
Woodland Community Primary School, Heywood

What Am I?

Makes the Earth hot like a burning pot.
Garbage builds up all the way to the top.
Killing all animals, which is sad, and you know it is bad!
Melting polar caps, now you won't understand your maps.
Destroying the ozone layer, don't make the sky greyer!
There will be no more snow and you don't want to know!
The water is rising as animals are surviving!
What am I?

Answer: Global warming.

Asiya Abiona (10)
Woodland Community Primary School, Heywood

The Effects Of Us

The more you drive,
The less everyone can thrive
The pollution in the air,
Is putting us in despair
But everyone is too busy to care

In the land of snow the more you smelt
The more you melt
Animals in the snow
Are struggling to grow
As they lie and cry
We laugh as they die

Walk and talk instead of drive
Then maybe the world will make it out alive
If you respect Earth it respects you.

Oliver Lyons-Butler (10)
Woodland Community Primary School, Heywood

I Remember When...

I remember when...
The ocean was a tsunami of happiness,
However, the chaos caught it.

I remember when...
The ocean was the heart of the Earth,
However, the murderer arrived and killed its soul.

I remember when...
The rainbow in the sea was beauty,
But then the poison cracked the dream.

I remember when...
The sea was a dream, but then the killer ended it for all.

Lucas Newton (10)
Woodland Community Primary School, Heywood

I Remember When...

I remember when...
The calm amazing ocean was the most liked area
Until an unstoppable devil came out of the blue.
I remember when...
You could see happy animals, but it did not last very long.
I remember...
How clean the water was,
The poor souls in the water are fading away.
I remember when...
The water was see-through,
At this point, the animals will go extinct.

Kaleb Innes (10)
Woodland Community Primary School, Heywood

What Have We Done?

Ice caps melt as you smelt,
Water will rise before your eyes,
We don't have time like somebody who has committed a crime.
Forests die as many cry,
On a hill eating meat not knowing what you kill,
All the factories you manage will cause damage.
All the fur coats made from polar bear,
You can buy a coat, not a polar bear,
Many mothers will cry as their sons and daughters die.

Leo Haycock (11)
Woodland Community Primary School, Heywood

Rainforest

R ain is often pitter-pattering here
A ll the bamboo is swaying softly
I n the tree sat a lonely toucan
N ot all trees can survive the deforestation
F rogs jumping full of glee
O rangutans swinging from tree to tree
R ain here is very heavy
E lephants stomping
S nakes hissing aggressively
T oucans sitting in the tree.

Kai Haslam
Woodland Community Primary School, Heywood

Wildlife

I live in the sea
The plastic is strangling me
I'm green
What am I?

Answer: A turtle.

I'm being cut down
I'm begging for them to stop
I have a lot of leaves
I have two colours
I produce oxygen
What am I?

Answer: A tree.

I am endangered
I'm grey
People want my horns
What am I?

Answer: A rhino.

George Heslop (9)
Woodland Community Primary School, Heywood

I Remember When...

I remember when...
The ocean was a sea of dreams,
However, now it's a living nightmare.

I remember when...
The world was a safe haven,
Until chaos struck the ocean.

I remember when...
The sea was a bubble of tranquillity,
However, the floating nightmare arrived.

I remember when...
It was heaven on earth,
Until the devil in disguise appeared.

Jenson-James Cooke (10)
Woodland Community Primary School, Heywood

The Rainforest

Tall trees and small bushes
Parrots mocking you in the trees.

Loud tasty raindrops falling off the trees
With an umbrella of leaves blocking the sunlight
The wet slippery vines with loud monkeys
Swinging across the trees.

Someone makes a warm cosy fire
All the animals come to see they are cold and want to keep warm.
So they go and stay near the fire.

Theodore (8)
Woodland Community Primary School, Heywood

Nature

People keep burning these trees down
It makes the trees start to cry and frown
It makes me cry
Because all I want
Is for some animals
To be happy and have nice homes
And all the animals start to run from their unfortunate, burnt-down homes
Nice and calm
I love the nature
When it's alive it makes me happy
And the trees dance and prance around happily.

Ayla
Woodland Community Primary School, Heywood

I Remember When...

I remember when...
It was paradise in the sea,
Then the killer of the sea came.
I remember when...
It was a sea full of dreams,
Now there's the king of devils.

I remember when...
It was safe and like heaven,
But now it's hell on earth.
I remember...
When it was the heart of the Earth,
Now it's the devil underwater.

Tommy Harman (10)
Woodland Community Primary School, Heywood

Forest Savers

R ain falls in the forest
A woodchopper chopping wood
I ndeed it's bad
N ever-ending pollution
F orests need our help
O ur help
R ainforests, river forests
E very forest needs our help
S ave all animals that live there
T oday you can make a change, we are the forest
S avers.

Robyn Murphy (8)
Woodland Community Primary School, Heywood

I Remember When...

I remember when...
The sea was a rage of peace,
But then came the devil in disguise.
It was a tsunami of happiness,
Now a devil underwater.

It makes me stressed, it makes me depressed
To see all them animals dying.

It used to be a dream like a perfect fantasy for the ocean and animals
But now it's not.

Alicja Roczen (10)
Woodland Community Primary School, Heywood

The Earth

Our clean, beautiful Earth...
Is dying!
The cute animals are starving and homeless...
Chop, chop, chop!
The trees are burning in the forests!

Shaniya Derbyshire
Woodland Community Primary School, Heywood

What Am I?

I am sometimes underwater and sometimes on land
But I am really endangered more than you think.
I am usually born in eggs and I hatch under sand.
I have a big shell on my back.
I need your help the plastic pollution is killing me.
What am I?

Answer: I am a turtle.

Anum Ansari (9)
Woodland Community Primary School, Heywood

Who Am I?

I sway, play and wave,
The wind pushes me one side to another,
I play with monkeys, sloths, birds and herds
Leaves fall off me and they roll around
I try to call them back but they can't hear a sound.
Then they just start to dance around.
Who am I?

Answer: A tree.

Anastasia Czyżewska (9)
Woodland Community Primary School, Heywood

Save The World!

Did you know the expensive designer coats you wear
Are made from the hair of the poor innocent polar bear?
As times go by birds will die
And no longer fly.
Stop pollution and do not litter
Think twice, it might save your life
Walk instead of driving to keep the animals alive.

Laceymai Maher
Woodland Community Primary School, Heywood

Save Nature

Rainforests are in great danger.
People are burning down trees which animals are living in
Such as birds and snakes.
I love animals and I hate when animals die
Because the trees that they are living in are being burnt down.
We need to help the world
Animals live in it too.

Katelyn Brewin (8)
Woodland Community Primary School, Heywood

Rainforest

R ain all around
A nimals crawling
I nsects on plants
N ature hiding in trees
F rogs jumping on lily pads
O n the plants, tiny spiders
R ain in the water
E mpty spaces where trees used to be
S quawking parrots
T igers munching and crunching.

Amelie Carey
Woodland Community Primary School, Heywood

Pollution

P lastic is bad for fish
O ne piece could choke a fish
L ove it or hate it,
L et's change it
U nder the sea
T ogether we can stop it
I f we stop littering, no more fish would die
O ne day all the fish could suffer
N obody should litter.

Harry Finn (9)
Woodland Community Primary School, Heywood

What Am I?

I come out at night
I eat meat
Also I eat bunnies' feet
I don't get fed quite a lot
But I like food quite a lot?
What am I?

Answer: A fox.

I am huge,
I eat grass,
Also you and I
Quite the same
But we are extinct
What am I?

Answer: A dinosaur.

Joshua Radcliffe (9)
Woodland Community Primary School, Heywood

I Remember When...

I remember when...
The world was clean and safe like heaven
Now it's dirty and disgusting
Since the devil arrived.
I remember when...
The happy fish were shining brightly from the twinkle of the hot sun
Now the murderer has killed the beautiful light.

Leo Lomax (10)
Woodland Community Primary School, Heywood

Our Planet, Earth

Our enormous clean planet is dying,
Because of... humans!
They are chopping trees down,
Chop, chop, chop!
They are throwing ugly litter
Smash, smash, smash!
The seas and oceans are smelly,
Because of... humans
Again!

Obed Lokongo (6)
Woodland Community Primary School, Heywood

Rainforest

Birds whistling through the tall trees
Air waving the grass, the blue sky watching us through the trees.
Sunlight crashing down on us like a plane
Green grass waving
Rainwater dropping smoothly
Cold air swooshing through the wavy tall trees.

Kozen Rostmay (8)
Woodland Community Primary School, Heywood

Big Green Planet

Disrupted by disgraceful, rude people
This Earth needs our help!
The animals are hurt, they need their families back
Thoughtful, kind trees give us fresh air
They need to be fresh, clean and green!
Please, if you litter, stop!

AvaRose Bayleigh Sierra Mintram (6)
Woodland Community Primary School, Heywood

Big, Green Planet

Our big, beautiful planet
People dropping stinky, awful rubbish
Change!
Ruined by greedy, smelly humans!
Fresh green trees cut down
Nasty, horrible oil burning
Needs our help
Sad, lonely animals losing their homes.

Zayan Ajaz (6)
Woodland Community Primary School, Heywood

Ocean Saver

O n the rocks the waves crash like a fierce lion.
C ould you name a fish? How about Ryan?
E ven sharks need help.
A ll of the kelp is rotting.
N obody should pollute because the fish are dying.
S ave our oceans.

Ava Mohammed (9)
Woodland Community Primary School, Heywood

Big Green Planet

Ruined by selfish, greedy humans
Dropping awful, disgusting litter
It needs our help
Sad, lonely animals are losing their homes
Fabulous green trees are cut down
Nasty, horrible oil burning
Earth needs our help.

Esme Moran
Woodland Community Primary School, Heywood

Big Green Planet

The big, beautiful Earth is being ruined by nasty, silly people
Cute, fluffy animals are dying because of it
Stinky, sticky rubbish is covering the lovely, fantastic planet
Lots of people are releasing harmful, dirty gases.

Sam Holt (7)
Woodland Community Primary School, Heywood

What Am I?

I live in the ocean
I'm very friendly
But I need your help as our species are melting away.
We put on a show for your entertainment.
Our babies are called calves
We are mammals.
What am I?

Answer: A dolphin.

George Taylor (10)
Woodland Community Primary School, Heywood

The Planet

Our planet is dying
Keep our planet safe and clean
Our planet is sad
Keep cleaning
Please make the dirty sea glistening and blue
Please leave the adorable animals alone
Help the Earth!
Help the Earth!

Lola Wyderska (6)
Woodland Community Primary School, Heywood

The Earth

Our amazing, clean Earth is dying
Broken, bent trees are falling down
Cut, cut, cut...
Plastic is going into the blue, smelly sea
Fish will die
The cute, adorable animals are starving, homeless and hungry.

Jack Harrison (7)
Woodland Community Primary School, Heywood

Fish

Fishes hiding from the animals that want to eat the fish,
Hoping they will not be found!

Thankfully the fish aren't found
Hopefully the sharks go away!

Outside the ocean is very windy,
At least the fish can't feel it!

Nelly Bialous (8)
Woodland Community Primary School, Heywood

Rainforest

Trees shaking, sloths snoring and footsteps creaking.
Monkeys climbing vine to vine
Parrots talking while bananas fly.
Waterfalls splashing like raindrops in the sky
Animals' homes are still alive.

Kaitlin Farrell (9)
Woodland Community Primary School, Heywood

The Ocean

O ctopus swimming side by side
C rocodiles nipping to eat you up
E els starving, wanting to have meat
A nimals choking on plastic
N o plastic, but they have already died.

Isla Bradley
Woodland Community Primary School, Heywood

Help The Ocean Stay Alive

O ceans are getting dirtier by every second.
C lean the ocean.
E veryone has one chance to help the ocean.
A lways throw your rubbish in the bin.
N o one should throw plastic in the water.

Oliver
Woodland Community Primary School, Heywood

What Am I?

I fly everywhere
But humans break my house
They use my house to build lots of things
I'm fluffy as a big fluff ball
It's hot in my fluff
It is big and tough
What am I?

Answer: A toucan.

Julia Bonkowska (8)
Woodland Community Primary School, Heywood

Big Green Planet

Our lovely, fantastic Earth
Hurt by nasty, mean people
Sad, lonely animals are falling in cracks
Need our help
The animals are dying
The Earth is sick
It is not fair on the Earth.

Charlie Howarth (7)
Woodland Community Primary School, Heywood

In The Rainforest

Up in the sky the birds are tweeting up high.
The sloths are sleeping on the trees
Softly leaves are falling all around.
Butterflies are flying everywhere.
Snakes are hissing on the ground.

Maizie Stubbs (8)
Woodland Community Primary School, Heywood

Big Green Planet

Our lovely, fantastic Earth needs our help
Dropping sticky rubbish
Tall green trees are cut down
Ruined by nasty, mean people
Horrible, nasty oil is burning
It needs our help!

Hollie Baker (7)
Woodland Community Primary School, Heywood

Earth

E veryone can help the planet,
A ll people can recycle,
R euse things when you can,
T ogether we can make the world better,
H elp the world.

Save the world!

Jacob Hamilton (9)
Woodland Community Primary School, Heywood

The Beach

I can see the floppy fish flopping.
I can hear the loud, annoying seagulls squawking.
I can smell the very salty water.
I can touch the dirty, soft sand.
I can taste the shelly, yellowy golden sand.

Charley Cass (9)
Woodland Community Primary School, Heywood

Plastic Pollution

The ocean used to shine in blue
But not now because of you
Reduce, reduce
Reuse, reuse, reuse
And recycle
If you do these three rules
We will live in peace with the animals.

Robin Gill (8)
Woodland Community Primary School, Heywood

Big Green Planet

This green, fresh Earth
Is not fresh anymore
It needs our help
Nasty, horrible people are dropping litter
We need to change that
Please help the Earth
Please do it now!

Freya Jackson (7)
Woodland Community Primary School, Heywood

The Earth

Our happy, amazing Earth
Is getting worse
The cute animals are dying
I am hearing...
Chop! Chop!
Oh no, I have to stop
Please stop it
You might kill more animals.

Zunaira (7)
Woodland Community Primary School, Heywood

The Ocean

In the ocean fish swim all around,
As a boat goes over with not much sound,
Remember, don't litter in the sea,
It doesn't help our Earth or the ocean, which is 'me'.

Olivia Butterfield (9)
Woodland Community Primary School, Heywood

The Whole World Sees

While an elephant grows,
A cheetah runs.

While a crocodile snaps,
A monkey screams.

While a shark bites,
A fish swims,

And the whole world sees.

Logan Vilter (10)
Woodland Community Primary School, Heywood

Big Green Planet

It is being destroyed by nasty, harmful humans
Dropping disgusting, hurtful litter
This Earth needs us
Tall, delightful trees are getting cut down
Nasty, dirty gas is burning.

Ismail Ansari
Woodland Community Primary School, Heywood

The Planet

Our old amazing planet is dying so quickly
The fluffy, cute animals are dying
Nasty people are chopping down green tall trees!
People are getting upset because animals are dying.

Isabelle Redford
Woodland Community Primary School, Heywood

The Earth

To save Earth
You should never leave the bright lights on
You will waste electricity
The planet needs help
The Earth is dirty
People are throwing litter on the floor.

Willow Barlow (7)
Woodland Community Primary School, Heywood

The Ocean

O cean has lots of plastic.
C lean the ocean.
E veryone has a chance to help the ocean.
A lways don't litter in the ocean.
N o littering in the ocean.

Salim Ouaach (9) & Marvellous
Woodland Community Primary School, Heywood

Our Earth

Our amazing, incredible Earth is dying!
Our tall green trees have been chopped to the ground!
On the Earth there are really cute animals
That are hungry and starving.

Alfie Hynes (6)
Woodland Community Primary School, Heywood

Our Earth

We are on Earth
If mean, sneaky people litter
Our Earth will die
People need to recycle
Save our massive, colourful Earth
Stop littering, humans!

Iyosayi Ogbebor Festus (7)
Woodland Community Primary School, Heywood

The Earth

Our incredible, amazing Earth is dying
Cute, fluffy animals are so, so sad
They don't have a home
They cannot eat anything
They are getting cold.

Ameliya Hughes (7)
Woodland Community Primary School, Heywood

What Am I?

I am as grey as the rain
I have fins like a plain
I love to swim and I never have a grin
I live all around and I flout like a cloud

Answer: A shark.

Ruby Williams (9)
Woodland Community Primary School, Heywood

What Am I?

Animals we eat,
Ravage ocean we swim in,
Taking our food kills us,
I live in the Arctic,
Climate change is impacting me.
What am I?

Answer: A polar bear.

Colby Smith (9)
Woodland Community Primary School, Heywood

Save The Fish

Scaly fish
Eating plastic
Maybe your plastic
That you use
Everything is plastic
Especially your food wrappers
And your clothes.

Charlotte
Woodland Community Primary School, Heywood

Big Green Planet

Our big round planet
Needs your help
The sad, lonely animals
Are losing their homes
The nasty oozing is burning
We need your help!

Lainey Jackson
Woodland Community Primary School, Heywood

Big Green Planet

Stop climate change
I know you need palm oil but it hurts animals
Cute, fluffy animals are losing their family
Please stop now!

Evie Murphy (7)
Woodland Community Primary School, Heywood

Tiger

T eeth so sharp
I ntelligent, big cats
G reat big claws
E at lots of meat
R uns very fast.

Teejay Smith (8)
Woodland Community Primary School, Heywood

The Earth

The incredible, massive Earth is dying
Cute, upset animals need help
Massive green trees are bending
Broken, bent trees.

Jamie Wellings (6)
Woodland Community Primary School, Heywood

Tiger

T eeth so sharp
I n the jungle
G reat big claws
E at lots of meat
R uns very fast.

Dylan Walsh (7)
Woodland Community Primary School, Heywood

Big Green Planet

The kangaroo is bouncing
The monkey is hurt
The monkey needs cheering up
The Earth is dirty and it needs our help.

Jessie Sutton (6)
Woodland Community Primary School, Heywood

The Sea

Splashing, tall waves
Calming, ginormous sea animals
Deep deep down
Never know what you'll come across
Green, wet seaweed.

Bobby Jo Corns (9)
Woodland Community Primary School, Heywood

Oceans

O ctopus
C lams
E els
A ll the beautiful fish
N ow save our sea
S ave the sharks.

Skyla Gordon (8)
Woodland Community Primary School, Heywood

Lions

L ooking for food
I ncredible, enormous lions
O ver the forest, they run
N owhere to be seen.

Skylar George (8), Nicoleta & Ella Hassan
Woodland Community Primary School, Heywood

Lion

L ying down
I nviting its prey
O n the prowl
N oisy roars.

Lok Ching Yan (7)
Woodland Community Primary School, Heywood

Lion

L ying down
I nviting its prey
O n the hunt
N oisy roars.

Gracie-Anne Curtis (7) & Kobie Keane
Woodland Community Primary School, Heywood

Leopard

A haiku

Leopard fighting prey
Running through the trees quickly
Black, spotty, soft skin.

Keeyan Pike (8)
Woodland Community Primary School, Heywood

Sloth

A haiku

Sloth slowly slides down
As slow as the slowest snail
Claws cling to the branch.

Lucy Hutchinson (7)
Woodland Community Primary School, Heywood

Polar Bear
A haiku

White bear breaks the ice
Looking desperately for fish
Soft, white, fluffy fur.

Nathan Barron (7)
Woodland Community Primary School, Heywood

Polar Bear
A haiku

Polar bears are white
Polar bears can break ice fast
Polar bears are strong.

Adam Hussain (7)
Woodland Community Primary School, Heywood

Panda
A haiku

Panda prancing high
Soft, spotty black and white fur
Likes eating bamboo.

Skyla-Hart Lee-Hampson (8)
Woodland Community Primary School, Heywood

Leopard
A haiku

Leopard hides hungry
Hunting for his food to eat
He grabs with his claws.

Carter Cleary (8)
Woodland Community Primary School, Heywood

Panda
A haiku

The panda is black
He likes to climb the bamboo
Chewing on green sticks.

Carson McKenzie (7)
Woodland Community Primary School, Heywood

Leopard
A haiku

Leopard lying down
Waiting for his food to come
Pouncing with his claws.

Eleanor Jupp (8)
Woodland Community Primary School, Heywood

Panda
A haiku

Calm, precious panda
Munching on the crunchy grass
Dreaming it survives.

Penny Sedgley (7)
Woodland Community Primary School, Heywood

Panda

A haiku

Panda petrified
Munch bamboo under pressure
Grey, black and white prey.

Matilda Sedgley (7)
Woodland Community Primary School, Heywood

Rhino
A haiku

Rhinos are heavy
With a huge horn on its nose
They make the same sound.

Kai Foster (7)
Woodland Community Primary School, Heywood

Leopard
A haiku

Leaping leopard hunts
Running quickly on the grass
Tearing apart meat.

Teca Riaquinda (8)
Woodland Community Primary School, Heywood

Gorilla
A haiku

Gorilla climbing
Munching plants and sitting down
Wish not endangered.

Zhayo McCarter (7)
Woodland Community Primary School, Heywood

Tiger
A haiku

Golden tiger fights
Just wants to stay alive here
Just in the jungle.

Rahma Abiona (7)
Woodland Community Primary School, Heywood

Gorilla
A haiku

Graceful gorilla
Climbing in the tall, big trees
Dreaming about home.

Isaac Curran-Leavy (8)
Woodland Community Primary School, Heywood

Panda

A haiku

Bamboo is tasty
Most black pandas are babies
Climbing lots of trees.

Thomas Lomax (8)
Woodland Community Primary School, Heywood

Panda
A haiku

Black and white panda
Chewing bamboo carefully
He loves soft bamboo.

Amelia Harding Green (8)
Woodland Community Primary School, Heywood

Polar Bear
A haiku

Polar bear dreaming
Swimming in the frozen lake
Dreaming to not die.

Vanessa Vasilache (8)
Woodland Community Primary School, Heywood

Polar Bear
A haiku

Polar bears freezing
Walking on the freezing ice
Melting ice slowly.

Lucas Fieldhouse (7)
Woodland Community Primary School, Heywood

Polar Bear
A haiku

Polar bear swimming
Stamping on the frosty ice
Polar bear dreaming.

Marcie Watson (8)
Woodland Community Primary School, Heywood

Panda
A haiku

Panda prancing high
Its fur is so snuggly
Climbing trees with ease.

Finley Dudley (7)
Woodland Community Primary School, Heywood

Panda
A haiku

Precious, black panda
Destroying bamboo slowly
Dreaming to not die.

Ryan Ghorbani (7)
Woodland Community Primary School, Heywood

Grizzly Bear

A haiku

Chewing on bamboo
He sees the talking people
Getting tons of food.

Felicity McGuirk (7)
Woodland Community Primary School, Heywood

Panda
A haiku

Panda prancing help
Because people crept around
To kill the panda.

Jack Davies (8)
Woodland Community Primary School, Heywood

Panda

A haiku

Pretty panda scared
The people taking pictures
Panda ignores them.

Olivia Carroll-McArdle (8)
Woodland Community Primary School, Heywood

Pandas

A haiku

Pandas are pretty
Pandas are prancing around
Pandas always dream.

Charlotte Egan (7)
Woodland Community Primary School, Heywood

Panda

A haiku

Pandas are praying
The wildlife needing our help
It is in danger.

Scarlett Curran-Quinn (8)
Woodland Community Primary School, Heywood

Pandas

A haiku

Pandas munching food
Pandas eating nice bamboo
Pandas in danger.

Jessica Gledhill (7)
Woodland Community Primary School, Heywood

Panda

A haiku

Pretty, soft panda
Its fur is soft and fluffy
Hoping not to die.

Benedict Nunn (7)
Woodland Community Primary School, Heywood

Gorilla
A haiku

Golden gorilla
Beats its big chest angrily
People-like, but not.

Maxwell Lindley (7)
Woodland Community Primary School, Heywood

Panda

A haiku

Pretty black panda
Sitting silently alone
Sitting in the woods.

Lottie Benson (7)
Woodland Community Primary School, Heywood

Panda

A haiku

Chewing on bamboo
Sitting silently alone
Black and white panda.

Dorcas Adebanjo (7)
Woodland Community Primary School, Heywood

Tiger
A haiku

Tiny, tough tiger
Roaring as loud as it can
King of the jungle.

Frankie Rowles (7)
Woodland Community Primary School, Heywood

Lion
A haiku

Scared lion prancing
At owner because he is
Starving and angry.

Olivia Sloane (8)
Woodland Community Primary School, Heywood

Gorilla

A haiku

Gorilla greedy
Strong enough to snap a tree
Eating to help him.

Oliver Bates (8)
Woodland Community Primary School, Heywood

Tiger
A haiku

Deadly killer cat
Stealthily stalking its prey
Terrible tiger.

Charlie Hoyle (8)
Woodland Community Primary School, Heywood

Cheetah

A haiku

Fluffy, calm cheetah
People were taking photos
He was curious.

Alayna Ansari (8)
Woodland Community Primary School, Heywood

Tiger
A haiku

Terrific tiger
Eating meat he caught today
Living in the wild.

Angus McGuire (7)
Woodland Community Primary School, Heywood

Elephant
A haiku

Angry elephant
Because they hate cameras
Then he was calm too.

Poppie Rowles (7)
Woodland Community Primary School, Heywood

Lion
A haiku

Lion lying low
Waiting for its prey to come
Deadly killer cat.

Temmy Edema (7)
Woodland Community Primary School, Heywood

Tiger
A haiku

Tigers are tired
Rapid running to its prey
Stripy and orange.

Rosie Needham (7)
Woodland Community Primary School, Heywood

Panda

A haiku

Fluffy, black panda
Eating bamboo happily
Hoping not to die.

Annabelle Jupp (8)
Woodland Community Primary School, Heywood

Tiger
A haiku

Tiger good today
Tiger is very stripy
Tiger likes sleeping.

Tiffany Burrows (7)
Woodland Community Primary School, Heywood

Rhino

A haiku

A rhino charging
At its prey ravenously
And it has a horn.

Aidan Starns (8)
Woodland Community Primary School, Heywood

Gorilla

A haiku

Gorilla climbing
Catching its soft bananas
Enormous belly.

Carl Orman (7)
Woodland Community Primary School, Heywood

Red Panda

A haiku

Beautiful panda
Not bothering anyone
Munching on bamboo.

Hebe Furtado Alves (7)
Woodland Community Primary School, Heywood

Climate Change

C rying animals in the Arctic
L onely animals with no homes
I t needs to stop
M ore people are coming with axes
A hard metal big balloon the colour of the grey moon
T ons of trees in lots of forests
E arth is getting hotter every year

C are is important for the world
H undreds of my friends have gone
A nd forests full of friendly frogs that have gone
N ow all that is left is pollution
G o on and help us stop climate change
E arth is going to die or else.

Joseff Jackson (10)
Ysgol Gymraeg Henllan, Henllan

Fire Poetry

I'm light red and yellow.
I'm extremely hot.
I'm feared from far faces.
I sometimes live in a volcano and erupt.
My burning hot self makes forest fires and melts ice.
I smell like smoke.
I taste like ashes.
You will feel warm if you go near me.
You will see burning.
You will hear crackling.
What am I?

Answer: Fire.

   W ildfire
   I smell like smoke
   L ots of people use me to roast marshmallows
   D oom is what you'll have if you step into a fire

F orest fire is what I like to make
I taste like ashes
R oast marshmallows on me
E ars hear the trees burning in a forest fire.

Rhodri Cotterill (8)
Ysgol Gymraeg Henllan, Henllan

Save The World!

The world is getting too hot,
Bad people are banned from breakwater bay.
The world is round and extraordinary
Like the BFG and like a circle.
Animals are part of life on Earth.
Too many people are littering.
The forest fires are too much for nature.
Creatures are in danger of extinction.
Save the world!

Noa Evans (9)
Ysgol Gymraeg Henllan, Henllan

Save The Trees

The fire burns me down to the ground until I cry.
The forest fire flickers flames which burn the trees down.
Soon the trees will all be gone.
Nothing left of the trees.
I can see black burning branches and I can hear the wood crackling.
Now the trees are all gone.

Efa Parkes (9)
Ysgol Gymraeg Henllan, Henllan

The Forest

The forest is full of fun.
Pollution is all around me.
All my friends have gone.
I am lonely.
The forest is on fire.
I'm frightened.
The flaming hot fire is fierce.
I'm sad.
I'm slowly disappearing.
Can you help to save the forest?

Erin Salusbury
Ysgol Gymraeg Henllan, Henllan

What Am I?

What am I?
I'm hot and sad
I'm big and bright and I can spread
I'm big and powerful
I'm also orange and yellow
I'm bright and I've got flames
I raise into the sky
Ash comes from me
I can be extremely hot
What am I?

Answer: Fire.

Megan Davies (9)
Ysgol Gymraeg Henllan, Henllan

What Am I?

I am massive
I blow wind
I make wind
I can power the world
I go round and round
I am sometimes in the sea
I am tall
Can you guess what I am?

Answer: A wind turbine.

Harvey Davies
Ysgol Gymraeg Henllan, Henllan

YOUNG WRITERS INFORMATION

We hope you have enjoyed reading this book – and that you will continue to in the coming years.

If you're the parent or family member of an enthusiastic poet or story writer, do visit our website **www.youngwriters.co.uk/subscribe** and sign up to receive news, competitions, writing challenges and tips, activities and much, much more! There's lots to keep budding writers motivated!

If you would like to order further copies of this book, or any of our other titles, then please give us a call or order via your online account.

Young Writers
Remus House
Coltsfoot Drive
Peterborough
PE2 9BF
(01733) 890066
info@youngwriters.co.uk

Join in the conversation!
Tips, news, giveaways and much more!

YoungWritersUK   YoungWritersCW   youngwriterscw

Scan me to watch The Big Green video!